FRED BASSET YEARBOOK 2024

An Hachette UK Company
www.hachette.co.uk

Summersdale Publishers Ltd
Part of Octopus Publishing Group Limited
Carmelite House
50 Victoria Embankment
LONDON
EC4Y 0DZ
UK

www.summersdale.com

Printed and bound in Poland

ISBN: 978-1-80007-980-9

2024

Didn't I do well?!

Substantial discounts on bulk quantities of Summersdale books are available to corporations, professional associations and other organisations.
For details contact general enquiries: telephone: +44 (0) 1243 771107 or email: enquiries@summersdale.com.